pasta
favourites

Your Promise of Success

Welcome to the world of Confident Cooking, created for you in our test kitchen, where recipes are double-tested by our team of home economists to achieve a high standard of success.

PERIPLUS

pasta favourites

Once upon a time, pasta was found only in Italy. But the secret is out and now the rest of the world enjoys pasta just as much as the Italians.

The beauty of pasta is that from such a simple base, an infinite variety of meals can be made. It adapts as easily to quick sauces as it does to long-simmering, thick ragus. This book includes a whole range of sauces to suit different tastes and time restraints, from a simple oil-based sauce that is ready in less time than it takes to cook the pastas to a hearty ragu. Included are classics such as Bolognese, Alfredo and Arrabiata; then there are sauces that blend new culinary ideas with the very Italian notions of simplicity and harmony.

which sauce goes best with what pasta?

It can be very confusing working out which sauce to serve with which pasta given that there is an astonishing variety of pasta on the market. As a basic rule of thumb, thick, chunky sauces are best served with tubular or spiral pastas so the sauce can nestle in the tunnels and grooves. Smooth sauces, which are generally cream and olive oil based, are best suited to long thin pastas, such as spaghetti or fettucine. Tiny pasta such as ditallini and stellini are usually used only in soups.

The pastas we have served with the sauces in this book are simply a guide to the most appropriate style of pasta, whether it be long and thin, short and curly, fresh or dried. However, there are no hard and fast rules and part of the fun of pasta is experimenting with different shapes, sizes and flavours.

fresh or dried?

Contrary to common opinion, fresh pasta is not necessarily superior to dried pasta. In fact, the two are treated very differently in cooking, and sauces that go with one do not necessarily go with the other. Fresh pasta is made with eggs and soft wheat 00 flour (*doppio zero*), whereas dried pasta is made out of durum wheat flour and water. Fresh pasta is more delicate and lighter than dried pasta and as such can tolerate richer sauces made from cream, butter and cheese. Dried pasta, on the other hand, is more often teamed with more rustic and robust sauces, such as those with olive oil, vegetable or meat bases.

how much pasta?

Because pasta varies so much in shape and weight it is difficult to be specific about how much pasta you will need per serve. The chart below gives some basic guidelines about how much pasta to provide per person.

	starter	*main*
fresh	85 g (3 oz)	140 g (5 oz)
dried	60 g (2¼ oz)	115 g (4 oz)
filled	125 g (4½ oz)	150 g (5½ oz)

Although it is traditionally served as a first course in Italy, elsewhere pasta is commonly eaten as a main dish. In recognition of this, most of the recipes in this book serve enough for a main meal. There are some exceptions (they are clearly marked) that are better as a light meal or first course because they are very rich and are best savoured in smaller portions.

not too much sauce

The amount of sauce you provide is a matter of personal taste, but the biggest mistake many people make when saucing the pasta is to add too much. The pasta should be just coated, not drenched.

how to cook pasta

Always cook pasta in a large pot in lots of salted, boiling water (about 1 litre/4 cups per 100 g/3½ oz pasta, more for filled pasta). Never use less than 1 litre (4 cups) water, even for small amounts of pasta. Keep the water at a rolling boil and stir the pasta once or twice to stop it clumping together. Adding a little oil to the water may prevent the pasta from sticking together, but this will make it slippery and harder for the sauce to stick. Cook the pasta until it is *al dente*, literally 'to the tooth' in Italian. Use the cooking instructions on the packet as a guide to the time needed, but the best way to check if it is cooked is to taste the pasta—it should retain a little bite. When the pasta is cooked, drain it in a colander, leaving a little water clinging to the pasta to stop it from sticking together. Either return the pasta to its cooking pan or add it to the sauce, but don't leave it sitting in the colander or it will clump together.

puttanesca

PREP TIME: 15 MINUTES
COOKING TIME: 20 MINUTES
SERVES 4

6 large ripe tomatoes
80 ml (1/3 cup) olive oil
2 onions, finely chopped
3 garlic cloves, finely chopped
1/2 teaspoon chilli flakes
4 tablespoons capers, rinsed and squeezed dry
7–8 anchovies in oil, drained and chopped
150 g (5 1/2 oz) Kalamata olives
3 tablespoons chopped flat-leaf (Italian) parsley

NUTRITION PER SERVE: Fat 19 g; Carbohydrate 18 g; Protein 6 g; Dietary Fibre 3 g; Cholesterol 6 mg; 1115 kJ (265 Cal)

1 Score a cross in the base of each tomato. Put the tomatoes in a bowl of boiling water for 30 seconds, then plunge into cold water and peel the skin away from the cross. Dice the tomato flesh.

2 Heat the oil in a saucepan, add the onion and cook over medium heat for 5 minutes. Add the garlic and chilli flakes, and cook for 30 seconds before adding the capers, anchovies and diced tomato. Simmer over low heat for 5–10 minutes, or until thick and pulpy. Stir in the olives and parsley.

3 Add the hot pasta to the sauce and toss through until well combined. Season with salt and freshly ground black pepper and serve immediately.

pasta We served this sauce with 375 g (13 oz) spaghetti.

carbonara

PREP TIME: 5 MINUTES
COOKING TIME: 10 MINUTES
SERVES 4–6

1 tablespoon olive oil
200 g (7 oz) piece pancetta, cut into long thin strips
6 egg yolks
200 ml (7 fl oz) thick (double/heavy) cream
75 g (3/4 cup) freshly grated Parmesan cheese

NUTRITION PER SERVE (6): Fat 28.5 g; Carbohydrate 1 g; Protein 14.5 g; Dietary Fibre 0 g; Cholesterol 248 mg; 1315 kJ (315 Cal)

1 Heat the oil in a frying pan and cook the pancetta over high heat for 6 minutes, or until crisp and golden. Remove with a slotted spoon and drain on paper towels.

2 Beat the egg yolks, cream and the Parmesan together in a bowl and season generously. Return the freshly cooked and drained pasta to its saucepan and pour the egg mixture over the pasta, tossing gently. Add the pancetta, then return the pan to very low heat and cook for 30–60 seconds, or until the sauce thickens and coats the pasta. Season with pepper and serve immediately.

pasta We used 400 g (14 oz) penne rigate with the carbonara sauce.

note Be careful not to cook the pasta over high heat once you have added the egg mixture, or the sauce risks being scrambled by the heat.

alfredo

PREP TIME: 5 MINUTES
COOKING TIME: 10 MINUTES
SERVES 4–6

90 g (3 1/4 oz) butter
150 g (1 1/2 cups) freshly grated Parmesan cheese
300 ml (10 1/2 fl oz) cream
2 tablespoons chopped marjoram

NUTRITION PER SERVE (6): Fat 41.5 g; Carbohydrate 1.5 g; Protein 10.5 g; Dietary Fibre 0 g; Cholesterol 130 mg; 1745 kJ (415 Cal)

1 Just before the pasta is cooked, melt the butter in a saucepan over low heat. Add the Parmesan cheese and cream and bring to the boil. Reduce the heat to low and simmer, stirring constantly, for 2 minutes, or until the sauce has thickened slightly.

2 Stir in the marjoram and season with salt and freshly ground black pepper. Toss the hot pasta through the sauce until well coated, then serve immediately.

pasta Try 650 g (1 lb 7 oz) filled pasta, such as veal agnolotti.

variation Marjoram is just one of many herbs that you could use. Try parsley, thyme, chervil or dill, and adjust the quantities to taste.

pictured: carbonara

bolognese

PREP TIME: 15 MINUTES
COOKING TIME: 3 HOURS 10 MINUTES
SERVES 4–6

2 tablespoons olive oil
2 garlic cloves, finely chopped
1 large onion, finely chopped
1 carrot, finely chopped
1 celery stalk, finely chopped
50 g (1 3/4 oz) pancetta, finely chopped
500 g (1 lb 2 oz) minced (ground) beef
500 ml (2 cups) beef stock
375 ml (1 1/2 cups) red wine
2 x 400 g (14 oz) cans chopped tomatoes
2 tablespoons tomato paste (purée)
1 teaspoon sugar
shaved Parmesan cheese, to serve

NUTRITION PER SERVE (6): Fat 13 g; Carbohydrate 9 g; Protein 21.5 g; Dietary Fibre 3 g; Cholesterol 47.5 mg; 1180 kJ (280 Cal)

1 Heat the oil in a large, deep saucepan. Add the garlic, onion, carrot, celery and pancetta and cook, stirring, over medium heat for about 5 minutes, or until softened.

2 Add the mince and break up any lumps with the back of a spoon, stirring until just browned. Add the stock, red wine, tomatoes, tomato paste and sugar. Bring to the boil, then reduce the heat to very low and simmer, covered, stirring occasionally, for 1 1/2 hours. Remove the lid and simmer, stirring occasionally, for a further 1 1/2 hours. Season to taste with salt and freshly ground pepper.

3 To serve, spoon the sauce over the hot pasta and sprinkle with some of the shaved Parmesan.

pasta We served the sauce with 500 g (1 lb 2 oz) fresh tagliatelle.

scallop, rocket and lemon

PREP TIME: 15 MINUTES
COOKING TIME: 15 MINUTES
SERVES 4

100 g (3½ oz) butter
3 garlic cloves, finely chopped
24 scallops, without roe
150 g (5½ oz) baby rocket (arugula) leaves
2 teaspoons finely grated lemon zest
60 ml (¼ cup) lemon juice
125 g (4½ oz) semi-dried (sun-blushed) tomatoes, thinly sliced

NUTRITION PER SERVE: Fat 20 g; Carbohydrate 13 g; Protein 14 g; Dietary Fibre 5.5 g; Cholesterol 80 mg; 1205 kJ (290 Cal)

1 Melt the butter in a small saucepan, add the garlic and cook over low heat, stirring, for 1 minute. Remove the pan from the heat.

2 Heat a lightly greased chargrill pan (griddle) over high heat. Lightly brush both sides of the scallops with the garlic butter and season with salt and pepper. When the chargrill pan is very hot, sear the scallops for 1 minute on each side, or until golden and just cooked through. Keep warm.

3 Toss the hot pasta with the rocket, lemon zest and juice, tomato and the remaining garlic butter until combined. Season. Divide among four bowls and top with the scallops.

pasta We used 350 g (12 oz) angel hair.

note Put the scallops on at the same time as the pasta.

crab, lemon and chilli

PREP TIME: 10 MINUTES
COOKING TIME: 10 MINUTES
SERVES 4–6

150 ml (5½ fl oz) virgin olive oil
2 small red chillies, seeded and finely chopped
3 garlic cloves, finely chopped
1½ teaspoons finely grated lemon zest
2 tablespoons finely chopped flat-leaf (Italian) parsley
1½ tablespoons chopped chives
500 g (1 lb 2 oz) fresh crab meat
60 ml (¼ cup) lemon juice
extra virgin olive oil, to drizzle (optional)

NUTRITION PER SERVE (6): Fat 21 g; Carbohydrate 1.5 g; Protein 11 g; Dietary Fibre 0.5 g; Cholesterol 70 mg; 995 kJ (235 Cal)

1 Pour the oil into a small saucepan, then add the chilli, garlic and ½ teaspoon of the lemon zest and stir over very low heat for 7–8 minutes to infuse the oil, or until the garlic is lightly golden—do not allow the oil to reach smoking point or the garlic will burn and taste bitter.

2 Put the hot pasta in a large bowl, pour on the infused oil and toss through until combined. Add the parsley, chives, crab meat, lemon juice and remaining lemon zest, and toss well. Season with salt and pepper and serve immediately. Drizzle with extra virgin olive oil, if desired.

pasta Try 500 g (1 lb 2 oz) spaghettini or other long, thin pasta.

pictured: scallop, rocket and lemon

classic pomodoro

PREP TIME: 10 MINUTES
COOKING TIME: 25 MINUTES
SERVES 4–6

60 ml (1/4 cup) olive oil
1 onion, finely chopped
3 garlic cloves, finely chopped
3 x 400 g (14 oz) cans chopped tomatoes
1 tablespoon tomato paste (purée)
bouquet garni
3 tablespoons torn basil leaves
freshly grated Parmesan cheese,
   to serve (optional)

NUTRITION PER SERVE (6): Fat 9.5 g; Carbohydrate 8 g; Protein 2 g; Dietary Fibre 3 g; Cholesterol 0 mg; 515 kJ (125 Cal)

1 Heat the oil in a deep frying pan and cook the onion over medium heat for 4–5 minutes, or until softened. Add the garlic and cook for 30 seconds before adding the tomato, tomato paste, bouquet garni and some salt and freshly ground black pepper. Reduce the heat to low and simmer for 15–20 minutes, or until the sauce thickens, stirring occasionally. Add the basil and, if the sauce is too tart, a pinch of sugar. Remove the bouquet garni.

2 Toss through the hot pasta and serve with grated Parmesan, if desired.

pasta We served the pomodoro sauce with 500 g (1 lb 2 oz) penne rigate.

variation To make a tomato and cream sauce, stir in 125 ml (1/2 cup) cream after removing the bouquet garni and simmer for a further 5 minutes.

slow-roasted tomato

PREP TIME: 15 MINUTES
COOKING TIME: 3 HOURS
SERVES 4–6

2 kg (4 lb 8 oz) ripe Roma (plum) tomatoes
1 large red onion, chopped
4 garlic cloves, finely chopped
1 tablespoon finely chopped thyme
2 teaspoons soft brown sugar
1 tablespoon good-quality balsamic
   vinegar (see Note)
80 ml (1/3 cup) olive oil
shaved Parmesan cheese, to serve

NUTRITION PER SERVE (6): Fat 12 g; Carbohydrate 8.5 g; Protein 3.5 g; Dietary Fibre 4.5 g; Cholesterol 0 mg; 665 kJ (160 Cal)

1 Preheat the oven to 180°C (350°F/Gas 4). Cut the tomatoes into large chunks and put them in a large roasting tin. Add the onion, garlic, thyme, sugar, vinegar, olive oil and a generous amount of salt and freshly ground black pepper, then toss together until well combined.

2 Roast the tomatoes, stirring every 20 minutes or so, for 2 1/2–3 hours, or until the tomatoes are slightly caramelized and breaking down to form a chunky sauce. Season to taste, then toss with the hot pasta. Sprinkle with some Parmesan before serving.

pasta When we tested this sauce, we used 500 g (1 lb 2 oz) penne rigate.

note Good-quality balsamic vinegar is always labelled aceto balsamico di Modena.

broccoli, anchovies and basil

PREP TIME: 15 MINUTES
COOKING TIME: 25 MINUTES
SERVES 4–6

600 g (1 lb 5 oz) broccoli, cut into florets
1 tablespoon olive oil
4 garlic cloves, finely chopped
8 anchovy fillets, roughly chopped
250 ml (1 cup) cream
30 g (1 cup) basil leaves, torn
2 teaspoons finely grated lemon zest
100 g (1 cup) freshly grated Parmesan cheese

NUTRITION PER SERVE (6): Fat 27 g; Carbohydrate 2 g; Protein 13.5 g; Dietary Fibre 4.5 g; Cholesterol 78 mg; 1270 kJ (305 Cal)

1 Cook the broccoli in a large saucepan of boiling salted water for 3–4 minutes. Remove with a slotted spoon and drain well.

2 Heat the oil in a frying pan. Add the garlic and anchovies and cook over medium heat for 1–2 minutes, or until the garlic begins to turn golden. Add the broccoli and cook for a further 5 minutes. Add the cream and half the basil and cook for 10 minutes, or until the cream has reduced and slightly thickened and the broccoli is very tender when tested with the point of a sharp knife.

3 Purée half the broccoli mixture in a food processor until nearly smooth, then return to the pan with the lemon zest, half the Parmesan and a little water, if necessary. Stir well, then season with salt and freshly ground black pepper. Add the hot pasta and the remaining basil to the pan and toss until well combined. Serve immediately with the remaining Parmesan sprinkled over the top.

pasta We used 500 g (1 lb 2 oz) orecchiette—any other pasta shape will work just as well.

roast chicken, pine nut and lemon

PREP TIME: 25 MINUTES
COOKING TIME: 1 HOUR 30 MINUTES
SERVES 4–6

1.3 kg (3 lb) chicken
1 bulb of garlic, cloves separated and left unpeeled
60 ml (1/4 cup) olive oil
30 g (1 oz) butter, softened
1 tablespoon finely chopped thyme
125 ml (1/2 cup) lemon juice
2 tablespoons currants
1 teaspoon finely grated lemon zest
50 g (1/3 cup) pine nuts, toasted
15 g (1/2 cup) finely chopped flat-leaf (Italian) parsley

NUTRITION PER SERVE (6): Fat 22 g; Carbohydrate 4.5 g; Protein 21.5 g; Dietary Fibre 2 g; Cholesterol 85.5 mg; 1275 kJ (305 Cal)

1 Preheat the oven to 200°C (400°F/Gas 6). Remove the neck from the inside of the chicken and place the neck in a roasting tin. Rinse the inside of the chicken with cold water and shake out any excess. Insert the garlic cloves into the cavity, then put the chicken in the roasting tin.

2 Combine the oil, butter, thyme and lemon juice, then rub all over the chicken. Season the chicken with salt and freshly ground black pepper. Roast for 1 hour, or until the skin is golden and the juices run clear when the chicken is pierced through the thigh with a skewer.

3 Transfer the chicken to a large bowl to catch any juices while resting. Remove the garlic from the cavity and leave until cool enough to handle. Squeeze the garlic cloves out of their skins, then finely chop.

4 Meanwhile, pour the juices from the roasting tin into a small saucepan and discard the neck. Add the currants, lemon zest and chopped garlic, then simmer gently over low heat while you remove all the meat from the chicken and shred into bite-size pieces. Add any of the resting juices to the pan.

5 Add the chicken meat, pine nuts, parsley and the sauce to the hot pasta and toss well. Season to taste with salt and pepper, then serve.

pasta We used 500 g (1 lb 2 oz) bavette but you can use other long, thin pasta, such as spaghetti.

prawns and leek in saffron cream

PREP TIME: 25 MINUTES
COOKING TIME: 35 MINUTES
SERVES 4–6 (AS A LIGHT MEAL)

40 g (1 1/2 oz) butter
1 small leek, julienned
4 garlic cloves, finely chopped
pinch of saffron threads
125 ml (1/2 cup) dry vermouth
250 ml (1 cup) fish stock
300 ml (10 1/2 fl oz) thick (double/heavy) cream
24 raw medium prawns (shrimp), peeled and deveined, with tails intact
1 tablespoon lemon juice
1 tablespoon finely chopped chervil, plus extra, to garnish (optional)

NUTRITION PER SERVE (6): Fat 24 g; Carbohydrate 3.5 g; Protein 12.5 g; Dietary Fibre 1 g; Cholesterol 148 mg; 1255 kJ (300 Cal)

1 Melt the butter in a saucepan over medium heat, add the leek and garlic and cook for 5 minutes, or until the leek is soft and translucent. Add the saffron, vermouth and fish stock and bring to the boil, skimming off any scum that rises to the surface. Reduce the heat to low and simmer for 10 minutes, or until it has reduced by half. Pour in the cream and simmer for 15 minutes, or until the sauce has thickened and reduced by about a third.

2 Add the prawns to the sauce and simmer for 2–3 minutes, or until cooked through. Remove from the heat and stir in the lemon juice and chervil. Season well, then toss through the hot pasta. Serve immediately, garnished with a little extra chervil, if desired.

pasta We used 400 g (14 oz) fresh tagliatelle, but there are many long, flat pastas that will be suitable.

note This dish is very rich and more suitable as a starter than a main course.

variation Parsley or dill can be used in place of chervil.

pumpkin and feta

PREP TIME: 15 MINUTES
COOKING TIME: 30 MINUTES
SERVES 4

1 kg (2 lb 4 oz) butternut pumpkin (squash), peeled and cut into 2 cm (3/4 inch) chunks
1 red onion, thinly sliced
8 garlic cloves, unpeeled
1 tablespoon rosemary leaves
80 ml (1/3 cup) olive oil
200 g (7 oz) marinated feta cheese, crumbled
2 tablespoons freshly grated Parmesan cheese
2 tablespoons finely chopped parsley

NUTRITION PER SERVE: Fat 30.5 g; Carbohydrate 11.5 g; Protein 13.5 g; Dietary Fibre 3.5 g; Cholesterol 37 mg; 1440 kJ (345 Cal)

1 Preheat the oven to 200°C (400°F/Gas 6). Put the pumpkin, onion, garlic and rosemary in a roasting tin, then drizzle with 1 tablespoon of the oil. Season. Using your hands, rub the oil onto all the ingredients until well coated. Roast for 30 minutes, or until the pumpkin is soft and starting to caramelize.

2 Squeeze the roasted garlic out of its skin and place it in a bowl with the remaining oil. Mash with a fork.

3 Add the garlic oil to the hot pasta, then the remaining ingredients. Toss well and season.

pasta We used 400 g (14 oz) casserechi pasta, but you could try macaroni or gemelli, or other short pasta.

pumpkin cream and thyme

PREP TIME: 15 MINUTES
COOKING TIME: 35 MINUTES
SERVES 4–6

1.3 kg (3 lb) butternut pumpkin (squash), peeled and cut into 2 cm (3/4 inch) chunks
4 garlic cloves, unpeeled
1 tablespoon thyme, plus extra, to garnish
2 tablespoons olive oil
60 ml (1/4 cup) cream
185 ml (3/4 cup) hot chicken stock
30 g (1 oz) shaved Parmesan cheese

NUTRITION PER SERVE (6): Fat 13 g; Carbohydrate 17 g; Protein 7.5 g; Dietary Fibre 3.5 g; Cholesterol 19 mg; 895 kJ (215 Cal)

1 Preheat the oven to 200°C (400°F/Gas 6). Put the pumpkin, garlic, thyme and oil in a bowl and toss together. Season with salt, transfer to a roasting tin and roast for 30 minutes, or until tender and golden.

2 Transfer the cooked pumpkin to a food processor or blender, pour in the cream and process until smooth. Add the hot stock and process until well blended. Season with salt and freshly ground black pepper. Gently toss through the hot pasta until well combined. Serve garnished with Parmesan and thyme.

pasta Serve with 500 g (1 lb 2 oz) pappardelle or other long, flat pasta.

pesto

PREP TIME: 10 MINUTES
COOKING TIME: NIL
SERVES 4–6

100 g (2 cups) firmly packed basil leaves
2 garlic cloves
40 g (¼ cup) pine nuts
185 ml (¾ cup) olive oil
50 g (½ cup) freshly grated Parmesan cheese, plus extra, to serve
2 tablespoons grated pecorino cheese

NUTRITION PER SERVE (6): Fat 36 g; Carbohydrate 0.5 g; Protein 6 g; Dietary Fibre 1 g; Cholesterol 12.5 mg; 1450 kJ (345 Cal)

1 Chop the basil, garlic, pine nuts and oil in a food processor with ¼ teaspoon salt until smooth. Transfer to a bowl and stir in the Parmesan and pecorino cheeses.

2 Reserve 2 tablespoons of the pasta cooking water and add to the pesto to make a smooth sauce. Toss with the hot pasta to coat well. Serve immediately with the extra Parmesan.

note Store any leftover pesto in an airtight jar for up to a week in the refrigerator. Completely cover the surface of the pesto with a layer of oil. It may also be frozen in the same way for up to 1 month.

pasta We used 500 g (1 lb 2 oz) linguine — you could try spaghetti or another long, thin pasta.

pesto rosso

PREP TIME: 10 MINUTES
COOKING TIME: NIL
SERVES 4

150 g (1 cup) sun-dried tomatoes, drained and finely chopped (reserving 1 tablespoon of the marinating oil)
100 g (½ cup) black olives, pitted and finely chopped
1 tablespoon tomato paste (purée)
1 garlic clove, finely chopped
2 teaspoons chopped thyme
½ teaspoon chilli flakes
80 ml (⅓ cup) virgin olive oil
50 g (½ cup) freshly grated Parmesan cheese, plus extra, to serve
3 tablespoons chopped parsley

NUTRITION PER SERVE: Fat 29 g; Carbohydrate 19 g; Protein 9.5 g; Dietary Fibre 6.5 g; Cholesterol 12 mg; 1565 kJ (375 Cal)

1 Combine the sun-dried tomatoes in a bowl with the olives, tomato paste, garlic, thyme and chilli flakes and season with salt and freshly ground black pepper. Add the olive oil and the reserved oil from the sun-dried tomatoes and mix thoroughly.

2 Reserve 2 tablespoons of the pasta cooking water and add to the pesto to make a smooth sauce. Toss with the hot pasta, then add the Parmesan and parsley. Combine well and serve with the extra Parmesan.

pasta Use 500 g (1 lb 2 oz) tortellini or other filled pasta.

amatriciana

PREP TIME: 10 MINUTES
COOKING TIME: 35 MINUTES
SERVES 4

2 tablespoons olive oil
200 g (7 oz) pancetta, thinly sliced
1 red onion, finely chopped
2 garlic cloves, finely chopped
1 teaspoon chilli flakes
2 teaspoons finely chopped rosemary
2 x 400 g (14 oz) cans chopped tomatoes
15 g (1/2 cup) chopped flat-leaf (Italian) parsley

NUTRITION PER SERVE: Fat 16.5 g; Carbohydrate 8 g; Protein 11.5 g; Dietary Fibre 3.5 g; Cholesterol 29 mg; 940 kJ (225 Cal)

1 Heat the oil in a frying pan and cook the pancetta over medium heat for 6–8 minutes, or until crisp. Add the onion, garlic, chilli flakes and rosemary and cook for a further 4–5 minutes, or until the onion has softened.

2 Add the tomato to the pan, season with salt and pepper, then bring to the boil. Reduce the heat to low and simmer for 20 minutes, or until the sauce is reduced and very thick.

3 Toss well with the hot pasta and parsley, then serve.

pasta We used 500 g (1 lb 2 oz) bucatini, but there are numerous other long, thin pastas to choose from.

arrabiata

PREP TIME: 5 MINUTES
COOKING TIME: 25 MINUTES
SERVES 4–6

2 tablespoons olive oil
4 garlic cloves, finely chopped
1 1/2 teaspoons chilli flakes
2 x 400 g (14 oz) cans chopped tomatoes
2 tablespoons chopped flat-leaf (Italian) parsley
freshly grated Parmesan cheese, to serve

NUTRITION PER SERVE (6): Fat 6.5 g; Carbohydrate 4.5 g; Protein 1.5 g; Dietary Fibre 2 g; Cholesterol 0 mg; 335 kJ (80 Cal)

1 Heat the oil in a saucepan over low heat. Add the garlic and chilli flakes and cook for 3–4 minutes, or until the garlic is lightly golden. Add the tomato, season with salt and simmer for 15–20 minutes, or until reduced and thick. Stir in the parsley and season to taste.

2 Add the hot pasta to the sauce and toss through until well combined. Serve immediately, sprinkled with Parmesan.

pasta Use 500 g (1 lb 2 oz) pasta shapes, such as penne or rigatoni.

tuna, caper, rocket and lemon

PREP TIME: 15 MINUTES
COOKING TIME: 5 MINUTES
SERVES 4

3 garlic cloves, crushed
1 teaspoon finely grated lemon zest
80 ml (1/3 cup) extra virgin olive oil
500 g (1 lb 2 oz) tuna, cut into 1.5 cm (5/8 inch) cubes
200 g (7 oz) rocket (arugula) leaves, washed, dried and roughly chopped
4 tablespoons baby capers in salt, rinsed and squeezed dry
60 ml (1/4 cup) lemon juice
2 tablespoons finely chopped flat-leaf (Italian) parsley

NUTRITION PER SERVE: Fat 24.5 g; Carbohydrate 3 g; Protein 33 g; Dietary Fibre 1.5 g; Cholesterol 45 mg; 1535 kJ (365 Cal)

1 Put the garlic, lemon zest and 1 tablespoon of the oil in a bowl with the tuna and gently mix. Season.

2 Heat a frying pan over high heat and sear the tuna for 30 seconds on each side. Add the rocket and capers, and gently stir for 1 minute, or until the rocket has just wilted. Pour in the lemon juice, then remove from the heat.

3 Add the remaining oil to the hot pasta along with the tuna mixture and parsley. Season to taste and gently toss. Serve immediately.

pasta We used 350 g (12 oz) fresh tagliarini — other pastas also come in thick ribbons.

tuna, oregano and creamy tomato

PREP TIME: 10 MINUTES
COOKING TIME: 20 MINUTES
SERVES 4–6

2 tablespoons olive oil
2 garlic cloves, finely chopped
2 x 400 g (14 oz) cans chopped tomatoes
2 teaspoons dried oregano
375 ml (1 1/2 cups) cream
300 g (10 1/2 oz) can tuna in oil, drained
2 teaspoons finely grated lemon zest
freshly grated Parmesan cheese, to serve (optional)

NUTRITION PER SERVE (6): Fat 38 g; Carbohydrate 6.5 g; Protein 10.5 g; Dietary Fibre 2 g; Cholesterol 99.5 mg; 1690 kJ (405 Cal)

1 Heat the oil in a saucepan over medium heat. Add the garlic and cook for 1–2 minutes, or until just starting to brown. Add the tomato and oregano, season lightly with salt and pepper, reduce the heat to low, then simmer for 12–15 minutes, or until the sauce has thickened and reduced.

2 Pour in the cream and simmer over low heat for 3–4 minutes. Gently stir in the tuna and lemon zest until combined. Season to taste. Add the hot pasta to the sauce and toss through until well combined. Serve with Parmesan, if desired.

pasta Use 500 g (1 lb 2 oz) penne rigate or other pasta shape.

pictured: tuna, caper, rocket and lemon

sage butter and shaved parmesan

PREP TIME: 5 MINUTES
COOKING TIME: 10 MINUTES
SERVES 4

200 g (7 oz) butter
16 sage leaves
shaved Parmesan cheese, to garnish

NUTRITION PER SERVE: Fat 35 g; Carbohydrate 0.5 g; Protein 0.5 g; Dietary Fibre 0 g; Cholesterol 109 mg; 1300 kJ (310 Cal)

1 Melt the butter over low heat in a small saucepan, without stirring or shaking. Carefully pour the clear butter into a bowl and discard the remaining white sediment.

2 Return the clarified butter to a clean pan and heat gently over medium heat. Add the sage leaves and cook until crisp but not brown. Remove and drain on paper towels. Reserve the warm butter.

3 Serve the hot pasta topped with the warm sage butter and leaves. Season with salt and pepper and garnish with shaved Parmesan.

pasta We used 375 g (13 oz) ravioli. This sauce is ideal for filled pastas such as ravioli, tortellini and agnolotti.

zucchini, ricotta and basil

PREP TIME: 15 MINUTES
COOKING TIME: 10 MINUTES
SERVES 4

60 ml (1/4 cup) olive oil
750 g (1 lb 10 oz) small zucchini (courgettes), thinly sliced
3 garlic cloves, finely chopped
350 g (12 oz) ricotta cheese, drained and crumbled
25 g (3/4 cup) basil leaves, torn, plus extra, to garnish
75 g (3/4 cup) coarsely grated Parmesan cheese, plus extra, to garnish
extra virgin olive oil, to serve

NUTRITION PER SERVE: Fat 27 g; Carbohydrate 2 g; Protein 13.5 g; Dietary Fibre 4.5 g; Cholesterol 78 g; 1270 kJ (305 Cal)

1 Heat the oil in a frying pan and cook the zucchini in two batches over high heat, tossing frequently, for 5–6 minutes, or until softened and golden brown. Add the garlic and toss for another 2–3 minutes, or until the garlic is lightly browned.

2 Add the hot pasta to the pan along with the ricotta, basil and Parmesan. Season to taste, and toss through until well combined. Drizzle with a little extra virgin olive oil and garnish with Parmesan and basil.

pasta Use 400 g (14 oz) gemelli or other twisted or shaped pasta.

cauliflower with bacon and pecorino

PREP TIME: 15 MINUTES
COOKING TIME: 20 MINUTES
SERVES 4

750 g (1 lb 10 oz) cauliflower, cut into florets
125 ml (1/2 cup) olive oil, plus extra, to drizzle
150 g (5 1/2 oz) bacon, diced
2 garlic cloves, finely chopped
80 g (1/2 cup) pine nuts, toasted
45 g (1/2 cup) grated pecorino cheese
15 g (1/2 cup) chopped flat-leaf (Italian) parsley
60 g (3/4 cup) fresh breadcrumbs, toasted

NUTRITION PER SERVE: Fat 55 g; Carbohydrate 15.5 g; Protein 18.5 g; Dietary Fibre 5.5 g; Cholesterol 32 mg; 2620 kJ (625 Cal)

1 Bring a large saucepan of boiling salted water to the boil and cook the cauliflower for 5–6 minutes, or until tender. Drain.

2 Heat the oil in a frying pan and cook the bacon over medium heat for 4–5 minutes, or until just crisp. Add the garlic and cook for 1 minute, or until just beginning to turn golden. Add the cauliflower and toss well.

3 Add the cooked pasta to the pan with the pine nuts, pecorino cheese, parsley and 40 g (1/2 cup) of the breadcrumbs and mix. Season; sprinkle with the remaining breadcrumbs and drizzle with a little extra oil.

pasta We used 500 g (1 lb 2 oz) orecchiette — little ears in Italian.

spinach, bacon and pecorino

PREP TIME: 15 MINUTES
COOKING TIME: 10 MINUTES
SERVES 4

80 ml (1/3 cup) olive oil
375 g (13 oz) bacon, cut into strips
3 garlic cloves, finely chopped
25 g (1 oz) butter, at room temperature
250 g (9 oz) baby English spinach, roughly chopped
90 g (1 cup) finely grated pecorino cheese
2 tablespoons chopped flat-leaf (Italian) parsley

NUTRITION PER SERVE: Fat 42.5 g; Carbohydrate 1 g; Protein 24.5 g; Dietary Fibre 2 g; Cholesterol 88 mg; 2005 kJ (480 Cal)

1 Heat 1 tablespoon of the oil in a large frying pan over medium heat. Add the bacon and cook for 6 minutes, or until crispy. Reduce the heat, add the garlic and cook for 3 minutes, then remove the pan from the heat.

2 Add the hot pasta to the pan along with the butter, spinach, pecorino, parsley and the remaining oil, stirring gently until the spinach wilts. Season to taste and serve immediately.

pasta Use 400 g (14 oz) fusilli, or other spiral-shaped pasta.

pictured: cauliflower with bacon and pecorino

lamb shank, rosemary and red wine ragu

PREP TIME: 25 MINUTES
COOKING TIME: 2 HOURS 45 MINUTES
SERVES 6–8

1 1/2 tablespoons olive oil
1 large onion, finely chopped
1 large carrot, finely diced
2 celery stalks, finely diced
2 bay leaves
1.5 kg (3 lb 5 oz) lamb shanks, trimmed of excess fat
4 garlic cloves, finely chopped
1 tablespoon finely chopped rosemary
750 ml (3 cups) dry red wine
1 litre (4 cups) beef stock
500 ml (2 cups) tomato passata
1/2 teaspoon finely grated lemon zest
flat-leaf (Italian) parsley leaves, to garnish

NUTRITION PER SERVE (8): Fat 16.5 g; Carbohydrate 9.5 g; Protein 43.5 g; Dietary Fibre 2 g; Cholesterol 137 mg; 1510 kJ (360 Cal)

1 Heat 1 tablespoon of the oil in a large, deep saucepan. Add the onion, carrot, celery and bay leaves and cook over medium–high heat, stirring often, for 8–10 minutes, or until the onion is lightly browned. Remove from the pan.

2 Heat a little more oil in the pan and cook the shanks in two batches, turning occasionally, for 15 minutes, or until browned all over. Remove from the pan.

3 Add the garlic and rosemary to the pan and cook for 30 seconds, or until lightly golden and fragrant. Return the vegetables to the pan, then stir in the red wine, stock, tomato passata, lemon zest and 250 ml (1 cup) water until combined. Using a wooden spoon, scrape up any sediment stuck to the base of the pan. Add the shanks and bring to the boil—carefully removing any scum that rises to the surface. Reduce the heat and simmer, uncovered, for 2 1/4 hours, or until the lamb is very tender and the sauce is thick and glossy.

4 Remove the shanks from the sauce and remove the meat from the bones using a fork and tongs. Discard the bones. Return the meat to the sauce and stir until heated through. Season. Add the hot pasta to the sauce and toss through until well combined. Serve garnished with parsley.

pasta We used 500 g (1 lb 2 oz) pappardelle, but you could try any pasta ribbon or cut strips out of lasagne sheets.

gorgonzola cream

PREP TIME: 5 MINUTES
COOKING TIME: 5 MINUTES
SERVES 4–6 (AS A LIGHT MEAL)

375 ml (1 1/2 cups) cream
200 g (7 oz) mild gorgonzola cheese, crumbled
2 tablespoons freshly grated Parmesan cheese
40 g (1 1/2 oz) butter
pinch of freshly grated nutmeg
toasted walnuts, broken up roughly, to garnish

NUTRITION PER SERVE (6): Fat 43.5 g; Carbohydrate 2 g; Protein 9 g; Dietary Fibre 0 g; Cholesterol 137 mg; 1795 kJ (430 Cal)

1 Put the cream, gorgonzola, Parmesan and butter in a saucepan and heat over low heat, stirring occasionally, for 3 minutes, or until the cheeses have melted into a smooth sauce.

2 Stir in the nutmeg and serve immediately over the hot pasta. Garnish with the walnuts.

pasta We used 500 g (1 lb 2 oz) ready-made potato gnocchi, which is available from supermarkets.

note This dish is very rich and is not recommended as a main course.

quattro formaggi (four cheeses)

PREP TIME: 10 MINUTES
COOKING TIME: 5 MINUTES
SERVES 4–6 (AS A LIGHT MEAL)

300 ml (10 1/2 fl oz) cream
40 g (1 1/2 oz) butter
100 g (1 cup) freshly grated Parmesan cheese (see Notes)
40 g (1/3 cup) freshly grated fontina cheese
75 g (1/3 cup) crumbled gorgonzola cheese
40 g (1/2 cup) grated provolone cheese

NUTRITION PER SERVE (6): Fat 40.5 g; Carbohydrate 1.5 g; Protein 13.5 g; Dietary Fibre 0 g; Cholesterol 128 mg; 1745 kJ (415 Cal)

1 Put the cream, butter, Parmesan, fontina, gorgonzola and provolone in a saucepan over low heat, stirring occasionally, for 3–4 minutes, or until the cheeses have melted into a rich and smooth sauce.

2 Season with salt and pepper and toss through the hot pasta until well combined.

pasta Use 375 g (13 oz) penne or other short pasta shape.

notes This dish is very rich and is not recommended as a main course.

It is important to use a good-quality Parmesan cheese such as Parmigiano Reggianno or Grana Padano. Grate the Parmesan yourself just before use, as the longer it is left grated, the less flavour remains.

pictured: gorgonzola cream

marinara

PREP TIME: 25 MINUTES
COOKING TIME: 1 HOUR 15 MINUTES
SERVES 4

1 tablespoon olive oil
1 onion, finely chopped
3 garlic cloves, finely chopped
2 x 400 g (14 oz) cans chopped tomatoes
2 tablespoons tomato paste (purée)
170 ml ($2/3$ cup) dry white wine
2 teaspoons soft brown sugar
1 teaspoon finely grated lemon zest
2 tablespoons torn basil leaves, plus extra, to garnish
2 tablespoons finely chopped flat-leaf (Italian) parsley
12 raw medium prawns (shrimp), peeled and deveined, tails intact
8 black mussels, scrubbed and beards removed
8 large white scallops, without roe
2 small squid tubes, cleaned and cut into 1 cm ($1/2$ inch) rings

NUTRITION PER SERVE: Fat 7 g; Carbohydrate 12.5 g; Protein 31 g; Dietary Fibre 4 g; Cholesterol 236.5 mg; 1120 kJ (270 Cal)

1 Heat the oil in a large saucepan, add the onion and cook over medium heat for 5–8 minutes, or until golden. Add the garlic, tomato, tomato paste, wine, sugar, lemon zest, 1 tablespoon of the basil, parsley and 250 ml (1 cup) water. Cook, stirring occasionally, for 1 hour, or until the sauce is reduced and thickened. Season.

2 Add the prawns and mussels and cook for 1 minute, then add the scallops and cook for a further 2 minutes. Stir in the squid and cook for 1 minute more, or until all the seafood is cooked through and tender.

3 Add the hot pasta to the sauce with the remaining basil and toss together until well combined. Serve immediately.

pasta We used 500 g (1 lb 2 oz) spaghetti, but any long, thin pasta will work well.

lentil, winter vegetable and thyme

PREP TIME: 10 MINUTES
COOKING TIME: 30 MINUTES
SERVES 4

1 litre (4 cups) chicken stock
2 tablespoons olive oil
1 onion, chopped
2 carrots, diced
3 celery stalks, diced
3 garlic cloves, finely chopped
1 1/2 tablespoons chopped thyme
400 g (14 oz) cooked green lentils (see Note)
virgin olive oil, to drizzle
freshly grated Parmesan cheese, to serve (optional)

NUTRITION PER SERVE: Fat 14 g; Carbohydrate 11 g; Protein 7 g; Dietary Fibre 4 g; Cholesterol 0 mg; 815 kJ (195 Cal)

1 Boil the chicken stock in a large saucepan for 10 minutes, or until reduced to 500 ml (2 cups) of liquid.

2 Heat the oil in a large, deep frying pan. Add the onion, carrot and celery and cook over medium heat for 10 minutes, or until browned. Add 2 cloves of the garlic and 1 tablespoon of the thyme and cook for a further minute. Pour in the stock, bring to the boil and cook for 8 minutes, or until reduced slightly and the vegetables are tender. Gently stir in the lentils until heated through.

3 Stir in the remaining garlic and thyme, and season with plenty of salt and freshly ground black pepper—the stock should be slightly syrupy at this point. Combine the hot pasta with the lentil sauce in a large bowl, drizzle generously with the extra oil and serve with grated Parmesan, if desired.

pasta We used 500 g (1 lb 2 oz) conchigliette (small shell pasta). Any other small pasta shape that can trap the sauce in its curves will work just as well; for example, orecchiette.

note If you don't want to cook the lentils yourself, use canned lentils.

artichoke, lemon and ham

PREP TIME: 15 MINUTES
COOKING TIME: 10 MINUTES
SERVES 4

25 g (1 oz) butter
2 large garlic cloves, finely chopped
150 g (5½ oz) marinated artichokes, drained and quartered
150 g (5½ oz) sliced leg ham, cut into strips
300 ml (10½ fl oz) cream
2 teaspoons finely grated lemon zest
15 g (½ cup) basil leaves, torn, plus extra, to garnish
35 g (⅓ cup) freshly grated Parmesan cheese, plus extra, to serve

NUTRITION PER SERVE: Fat 42.5 g; Carbohydrate 3 g; Protein 12.5 g; Dietary Fibre 1.5 g; Cholesterol 147 mg; 1840 kJ (440 Cal)

1 Melt the butter in a large frying pan over medium heat, then cook the garlic for 1 minute, or until fragrant. Add the artichokes and ham and cook for a further 2 minutes. Stir in the cream and lemon zest, reduce the heat and simmer for 5 minutes, gently breaking up the artichoke with a wooden spoon.

2 Pour the sauce over the hot pasta (which has been returned to its pan), then add the basil and Parmesan and toss. Season, garnish with basil and serve with extra Parmesan.

pasta We used 500 g (1 lb 2 oz) fresh linguine—try any fresh, ribboned pasta, such as tagliatelle.

creamy lemon

PREP TIME: 5 MINUTES
COOKING TIME: 5 MINUTES
SERVES 4–6 (AS A LIGHT MEAL)

60 g (2¼ oz) butter
250 ml (1 cup) thick (double/heavy) cream
60 ml (¼ cup) lemon juice
2 teaspoons finely grated lemon zest
15 g (½ cup) roughly chopped flat-leaf (Italian) parsley
50 g (½ cup) freshly grated Parmesan cheese

NUTRITION PER SERVE (6): Fat 26 g; Carbohydrate 1.5 g; Protein 4 g; Dietary Fibre 0 g; Cholesterol 80 mg; 1065 kJ (255 Cal)

1 Put the butter, cream, lemon juice and 1 teaspoon of the zest in a saucepan and simmer over medium heat for 3–4 minutes. Stir in the remaining zest and season.

2 Add the hot pasta to the sauce, along with the parsley and 25 g (¼ cup) of the Parmesan cheese and toss well. Serve immediately, sprinkled with the remaining Parmesan.

pasta Use 300 g (10½ oz) fresh tagliarini or other fresh pasta. Fresh pasta is best for this rich sauce because it is less heavy than dried.

note Rich sauces such as this one are more suited for serving in smaller portions as a first course or light meal.

meatball and tomato

PREP TIME: 30 MINUTES
COOKING TIME: 50 MINUTES
SERVES 6

Meatballs
2 slices white bread, crusts removed
60 ml (1/4 cup) milk
500 g (1 lb 2 oz) minced (ground) pork and veal (see Note)
1 small onion, finely chopped
2 garlic cloves, finely chopped
3 tablespoons finely chopped flat-leaf (Italian) parsley
2 teaspoons finely grated lemon zest
1 egg, lightly beaten
50 g (1/2 cup) freshly grated Parmesan cheese
plain (all-purpose) flour, to coat
2 tablespoons olive oil

125 ml (1/2 cup) white wine
2 x 400 g (14 oz) cans chopped tomatoes
1 tablespoon tomato paste (purée)
1 teaspoon caster (superfine) sugar
1/2 teaspoon dried oregano
oregano leaves, to garnish

NUTRITION PER SERVE: Fat 15.5 g; Carbohydrate 13 g; Protein 24.5 g; Dietary Fibre 2.5 g; Cholesterol 102 mg; 1275 kJ (305 Cal)

1 To make the meatballs, soak the bread in the milk for 5 minutes, then squeeze out any moisture with your hands. Put the bread, mince, onion, garlic, parsley, lemon zest, egg and Parmesan in a large bowl, season and mix thoroughly with your hands.

2 Shape into walnut-size balls using damp hands, then roll lightly in the flour. Heat the oil in a large, deep frying pan and cook the meatballs in batches over medium heat, turning frequently, for 10 minutes, or until brown all over. Remove with a slotted spoon and drain on paper towels.

3 Pour the wine into the same frying pan and boil over medium heat for 2–3 minutes, or until it evaporates a little. Add the tomato, tomato paste, sugar and dried oregano. Reduce the heat to low, then simmer for 20 minutes, or until the sauce thickens and reduces. Add the meatballs and simmer for a further 10 minutes.

4 To serve, divide the hot pasta among six serving plates and spoon some meatballs and sauce over the top of each. Garnish with the fresh oregano and serve immediately.

pasta We used 500 g (1 lb 2 oz) penne rigate, which is essentially penne with ridges on the outside.

note You can use minced beef instead of the pork and veal, if you prefer.

squid in black ink

PREP TIME: 30 MINUTES
COOKING TIME: 1 HOUR 10 MINUTES
SERVES 4–6

1 kg (2 lb 4 oz) medium squid
2 tablespoons olive oil
1 onion, finely chopped
6 garlic cloves, finely chopped
1 bay leaf
1 small red chilli, seeded and thinly sliced
80 ml ($1/3$ cup) white wine
80 ml ($1/3$ cup) dry vermouth
250 ml (1 cup) fish stock
60 g ($1/4$ cup) tomato paste (purée)
500 ml (2 cups) tomato passata
15 g ($1/2$ oz) squid ink (see Note)
$1/2$ teaspoon Pernod (optional)
4 tablespoons chopped flat-leaf (Italian) parsley
1 garlic clove, extra, crushed

NUTRITION PER SERVE (6): Fat 7.5 g; Carbohydrate 12.5 g; Protein 21.5 g; Dietary Fibre 3 g; Cholesterol 216 mg; 955 kJ (230 Cal)

1 To clean the squid, gently pull the tentacles away from the hood (the intestines should come away at the same time). Remove the intestines from the tentacles by cutting under the eyes, then remove the beak if it remains in the centre of the tentacles by using your fingers to push up the centre. Pull away the quill (the transparent cartilage) from inside the body and discard. Remove and discard any white membrane. Cut the squid into thin slices.

2 Heat the oil in a saucepan over medium heat, then add the onion and cook for 8 minutes, or until lightly golden. Add the garlic, bay leaf and chilli and cook for a further 2 minutes, or until the garlic is lightly golden.

3 Stir in the wine, vermouth, fish stock, tomato paste, tomato passata and 250 ml (1 cup) water, then increase the heat to high and bring to the boil. Reduce to a simmer and cook for 45 minutes, or until the liquid has reduced by half. Add the squid ink and cook for a further 2 minutes, or until the sauce is evenly black and glossy.

4 Add the squid rings and Pernod, stir well, then cook for 4–5 minutes, or until they turn opaque and are cooked through and tender. Stir in the parsley and the extra garlic and season to taste. Toss through the hot pasta and serve immediately.

pasta We have used 500 g (1 lb 2 oz) spaghettini, which is slightly thinner than spaghetti.

note Squid ink is available in jars and sachets from gourmet food stores.

norma

PREP TIME: 15 MINUTES
COOKING TIME: 40 MINUTES
SERVES 4–6

185 ml (³/₄ cup) olive oil
1 onion, finely chopped
2 garlic cloves, finely chopped
2 x 400 g (14 oz) cans chopped tomatoes
1 large eggplant (aubergine)
   (about 500 g/1 lb 2 oz)
30 g (¹/₂ cup) basil leaves, torn, plus extra, to garnish
60 g (¹/₂ cup) ricotta salata (see Note), crumbled
45 g (¹/₂ cup) freshly grated pecorino or Parmesan cheese
1 tablespoon extra virgin olive oil, to drizzle

NUTRITION PER SERVE (6): Fat 29.5 g; Carbohydrate 7.5 g; Protein 6 g; Dietary Fibre 4 g; Cholesterol 12.5 mg; 1335 kJ (320 Cal)

1 Heat 2 tablespoons of the oil in a frying pan and cook the onion over medium heat for 5 minutes, or until softened. Stir in the garlic and cook for 30 seconds. Add the tomato and season to taste. Reduce the heat to low and cook for 20–25 minutes, or until the sauce has thickened and reduced.

2 Meanwhile, cut the eggplant lengthways into 5 mm (¹/₄ inch) thick slices. Heat the remaining olive oil in a large frying pan. When the oil is hot but not smoking, add the eggplant slices a few at a time and cook for 3–5 minutes, or until lightly browned on both sides. Remove from the pan and drain well on crumpled paper towels.

3 Add the eggplant to the sauce with the basil, stirring over very low heat.

4 Add the hot pasta to the sauce with half each of the ricotta and pecorino and toss together well. Serve immediately, sprinkled with the remaining cheeses and extra basil and drizzled with oil.

pasta We used 400 g (14 oz) bucatini, which is similar to spaghetti, but with a hollow centre that helps it cook more quickly than spaghetti.

note Ricotta salata is a lightly salted, pressed ricotta cheese. If unavailable, use a mild feta cheese.

boscaiola

PREP TIME: 10 MINUTES
COOKING TIME: 30 MINUTES
SERVES 4–6

30 g (1 oz) butter
4 rashers bacon, diced
2 garlic cloves, finely chopped
300 g (10 1/2 oz) Swiss brown or button mushrooms, sliced
60 ml (1/4 cup) dry white wine
375 ml (1 1/2 cups) cream
1 teaspoon chopped thyme
50 g (1/2 cup) freshly grated Parmesan cheese
1 tablespoon chopped flat-leaf (Italian) parsley

NUTRITION PER SERVE (6): Fat 41 g; Carbohydrate 3 g; Protein 12.5 g; Dietary Fibre 1.5 g; Cholesterol 127 mg; 1800 kJ (430 Cal)

1 Melt the butter in a large frying pan, add the bacon and cook over medium heat for 5 minutes, or until crisp. Add the garlic and cook for 2 minutes, then add the mushrooms, cooking for a further 8 minutes, or until softened. Stir in the wine and cream and add the thyme and bring to the boil. Reduce the heat to low and simmer for 10 minutes, or until the sauce has thickened.

2 Combine the sauce with the hot pasta, Parmesan and parsley. Season to taste and serve immediately.

pasta We used 500 g (1 lb 2 oz) veal tortellini, the name of which is said to refer to Venus' navel.

creamy mushroom

PREP TIME: 10 MINUTES
COOKING TIME: 20 MINUTES
SERVES 4

30 g (1 oz) butter
1 tablespoon olive oil
600 g (1 lb 5 oz) Swiss brown or small field mushrooms, thinly sliced
3 garlic cloves, finely chopped
1 tablespoon chopped thyme
125 ml (1/2 cup) dry white wine
300 ml (10 1/2 fl oz) thick (double/heavy) cream
3 tablespoons chopped flat-leaf (Italian) parsley
25 g (1/4 cup) freshly grated Parmesan cheese

NUTRITION PER SERVE: Fat 40 g; Carbohydrate 5 g; Protein 9.5 g; Dietary Fibre 4.5 g; Cholesterol 110 mg; 1820 kJ (435 Cal)

1 Heat the butter and oil in a frying pan over high heat. When the butter begins to foam, add the mushrooms and cook, stirring frequently, for 5 minutes, or until lightly browned.

2 Add the garlic and thyme, season with salt and pepper and cook for 1 minute. Pour in the wine and simmer for 5 minutes, or until the liquid is nearly evaporated. Add the cream and cook for 5 minutes, or until the sauce thickens and reduces a little. Toss the sauce through the cooked pasta with the parsley and Parmesan.

pasta Use 500 g (1 lb 2 oz) veal tortellini or other stuffed pasta.

anchovy, caper and chilli

PREP TIME: 15 MINUTES
COOKING TIME: 5 MINUTES
SERVES 4

125 ml (1/2 cup) olive oil
4 garlic cloves, finely chopped
10 anchovy fillets, chopped
1 tablespoon baby capers, rinsed and squeezed dry
1 teaspoon chilli flakes
2 tablespoons lemon juice
2 teaspoons finely grated lemon zest
3 tablespoons chopped parsley
3 tablespoons chopped basil leaves
3 tablespoons chopped mint
50 g (1/2 cup) coarsely grated Parmesan cheese, plus extra, to serve
extra virgin olive oil, to drizzle

NUTRITION PER SERVE: Fat 33 g; Carbohydrate 1 g; Protein 7.5 g; Dietary Fibre 1 g; Cholesterol 18.5 mg; 1375 kJ (330 Cal)

1 Heat the oil in a frying pan and cook the garlic over medium heat for 2–3 minutes, or until starting to brown. Add the anchovies, capers and chilli flakes and cook for a further minute.

2 Add the hot pasta to the pan with the lemon juice, lemon zest, parsley, basil, mint and Parmesan. Season to taste with salt and pepper and toss together well.

3 To serve, drizzle with a little extra oil and sprinkle with Parmesan.

pasta We have used 400 g (14 oz) spaghettini, which are 'little lengths of cord' even thinner than spaghetti.

pictured: anchovy, caper and chilli

rocket, fresh tomato and parmesan

PREP TIME: 20 MINUTES
COOKING TIME: 10 MINUTES
SERVES 4

1 kg (2 lb 4 oz) ripe Roma (plum) tomatoes
80 ml (1/3 cup) olive oil
3 garlic cloves, finely chopped
2 tablespoons finely chopped flat-leaf (Italian) parsley
100 g (3 1/2 oz) baby rocket (arugula) leaves
70 g (2 1/2 oz) Parmesan cheese, shaved

NUTRITION PER SERVE: Fat 24 g; Carbohydrate 5 g; Protein 10 g; Dietary Fibre 3.5 g; Cholesterol 16.5 mg; 1145 kJ (275 Cal)

1 Score a cross in the base of each tomato, then place in a large bowl. Cover with boiling water and stand for 1 minute. Remove the tomatoes, plunge into cold water, then peel the skin away from the cross. Remove the seeds and finely chop the flesh.

2 Heat the oil in a saucepan over medium heat. Add the garlic and cook for 1 minute, or until just starting to become golden, then add the tomato. Season well with salt and pepper. Reduce the heat to low and cook the tomato for 5–6 minutes, or until just warmed through. Stir in the parsley.

3 Add the tomato and rocket to the hot pasta and toss well. Serve, garnished with the shaved Parmesan.

pasta Use 400 g (14 oz) spaghettini or other long, thin pasta, such as vermicelli.

chicken, mushroom and tarragon

PREP TIME: 20 MINUTES
COOKING TIME: 25 MINUTES
SERVES 4

2 tablespoons virgin olive oil
350 g (12 oz) chicken tenderloins, cut into 2 cm (³/₄ inch) pieces
20 g (1 oz) butter
400 g (14 oz) Swiss brown or button mushrooms, sliced
2 garlic cloves, finely chopped
125 ml (¹/₂ cup) dry white wine
185 ml (³/₄ cup) cream
1 teaspoon finely grated lemon zest
2 tablespoons lemon juice
1 tablespoon chopped tarragon
2 tablespoons chopped parsley
25 g (¹/₄ cup) freshly grated Parmesan cheese, plus extra, to serve

NUTRITION PER SERVE: Fat 41.5 g; Carbohydrate 3.5 g; Protein 24 g; Dietary Fibre 3 g; Cholesterol 160.5 mg; 2085 kJ (500 Cal)

1 Heat 1 tablespoon of the oil in a large frying pan, add the chicken and cook over high heat for 3–4 minutes, or until lightly browned. Remove.

2 Heat the butter and the remaining oil, add the mushrooms and cook, stirring, over high heat for 3 minutes. Add the garlic and cook for a further 2 minutes.

3 Pour in the wine, then reduce the heat to low and simmer for 5 minutes, or until nearly evaporated. Add the cream and chicken, then simmer for about 5 minutes, or until thickened.

4 Stir the lemon zest, lemon juice, tarragon, parsley and Parmesan into the sauce. Season with salt and pepper, then add the hot pasta, tossing until well combined. Serve with the remaining Parmesan.

pasta We used 375 g (13 oz) fusilli, but there are any number of pasta shapes that can be used instead. Try ruote, conchiglie or penne.

sardine, fennel and pine nut

PREP TIME: 15 MINUTES +
  10 MINUTES SOAKING
COOKING TIME: 25 MINUTES
SERVES 4

60 g (¼ cup) currants
1 fennel bulb
80 ml (⅓ cup) olive oil, plus extra, for shallow-frying
1 red onion, finely chopped
½ teaspoon saffron threads, soaked in 1 tablespoon warm water
40 g (¼ cup) pine nuts, toasted
8 anchovy fillets, chopped
1 tablespoon tomato paste (purée)
350 g (12 oz) butterflied sardine fillets
plain (all-purpose) flour, to dust
40 g (½ cup) fresh breadcrumbs, toasted

NUTRITION PER SERVE: Fat 33 g; Carbohydrate 20 g; Protein 24.5 g; Dietary Fibre 4 g; Cholesterol 58 mg; 1960 kJ (470 Cal)

1 Cover the currants with warm water and allow to soak for 10 minutes. Drain well. Trim the tough outer leaves from the fennel bulb (reserving the fronds), then cut into quarters. Slice each quarter thinly and chop 2 tablespoons of the fronds.

2 Heat the oil in a frying pan. Cook the onion and fennel over low heat for 8–9 minutes, or until soft and tender. Add the currants, saffron, pine nuts and anchovies and cook for 3 minutes. Combine the tomato paste with 60 ml (¼ cup) water, add to the pan and simmer for 5 minutes.

3 Meanwhile, lightly dust the sardine fillets in flour, shaking off the excess. Heat a frying pan over medium heat with just enough oil to cover the bottom of the pan. Cook the sardines in batches for 1 minute on both sides, or until lightly golden and just cooked through. Drain on paper towels. Slice the sardines in half lengthways to give two fillets.

4 Toss the hot pasta through the fennel mixture until well combined. Season to taste, then stir in two-thirds of the sardines. Transfer to a serving bowl and arrange the remaining sardines on top. Sprinkle with the toasted breadcrumbs and fennel fronds.

pasta We used 400 g (14 oz) bucatini. Any of the long thin pastas can be used instead, such as spaghetti or bavette.

grilled capsicum

PREP TIME: 15 MINUTES
COOKING TIME: 15 MINUTES
SERVES 4–6

6 large red capsicums (peppers), halved
2 tablespoons olive oil
1 onion, thinly sliced
3 garlic cloves, finely chopped
2 tablespoons shredded basil leaves
whole basil leaves, to garnish
shaved Parmesan cheese, to serve

NUTRITION PER SERVE (6): Fat 6 g; Carbohydrate 5.5 g; Protein 2 g; Dietary Fibre 1 g; Cholesterol 0 mg; 355 kJ (85 Cal)

1 Cut the capsicums into large flattish pieces. Cook, skin-side-up, under a hot grill until the skin blackens and blisters. Place in a plastic bag and leave to cool, then peel the skin.

2 Heat the oil in a large frying pan, add the onion and garlic and cook over medium heat for 5 minutes, or until soft. Cut one capsicum into thin strips, then add to the onion mixture.

3 Chop the remaining capsicum, then purée in a food processor until smooth. Add to the onion mixture and cook over low heat for 5 minutes, or until warmed through.

4 Toss the sauce through the hot pasta. Season, then stir in the shredded basil. Garnish with the basil leaves and serve with the Parmesan.

pasta We used 400 g (14 oz) pasta gnocchi. You could try any pasta shape, such as rigatoni or conchiglie.

spicy sausage and tomato

PREP TIME: 10 MINUTES
COOKING TIME: 1 HOUR
SERVES 4

2 tablespoons olive oil
1 onion, finely chopped
2 garlic cloves, finely chopped
1 teaspoon chilli flakes
450 g (1 lb) Italian pork sausages, skin removed, cut into 1 cm ($1/2$ inch) lengths
1 teaspoon tomato paste (purée)
80 ml ($1/3$ cup) red wine
80 ml ($1/3$ cup) chicken stock
400 g (14 oz) can chopped tomatoes
3 tablespoons basil leaves, roughly torn
freshly grated Parmesan cheese, to serve

NUTRITION PER SERVE: Fat 34.5 g; Carbohydrate 8.5 g; Protein 15 g; Dietary Fibre 3.5 g; Cholesterol 73 mg; 1735 kJ (415 Cal)

1 Heat a frying pan over medium heat and add the oil. Add the onion, garlic and chilli flakes and cook for 5 minutes, or until soft. Add the sausage meat and cook for 8 minutes, or until the meat is well browned. Stir in the tomato paste and cook for 3 minutes.

2 Pour in the wine and cook for 5 minutes, or until reduced. Add the stock and tomato and simmer, covered, over very low heat for 45 minutes. Season well to taste.

3 Put the hot pasta in a bowl, add the sauce and basil and toss well. Serve with Parmesan.

pasta Use 400 g (14 oz) pasta gnocchi.

pictured: grilled capsicum

primavera

PREP TIME: 15 MINUTES
COOKING TIME: 10 MINUTES
SERVES 4–6

220 g (1¼ cups) fresh or frozen broad (fava) beans (see Note)
200 g (7 oz) asparagus spears, trimmed and cut into 5 cm (2 inch) pieces
235 g (1½ cups) peas, fresh or frozen
100 g (3½ oz) green beans, trimmed and cut into 3 cm (1¼ inch) pieces
30 g (1 oz) butter
3 spring onions (scallions), cut into 3 cm (1¼ inch) pieces
3 tablespoons chopped flat-leaf (Italian) parsley
300 ml (10½ fl oz) cream
50 g (½ cup) freshly grated Parmesan cheese

NUTRITION PER SERVE (6): Fat 28.5 g; Carbohydrate 9 g; Protein 10.5 g; Dietary Fibre 5 g; Cholesterol 89 mg; 1385 kJ (330 Cal)

1 Blanch the broad beans in a saucepan of boiling water for 1 minute, then add the asparagus, peas and green beans. Return to the boil and blanch the vegetables for 2 minutes, or until bright green and tender. Cool quickly under cold water and drain. Peel the broad beans.

2 Heat the butter in a large frying pan. Add the spring onion and cook for 2 minutes, then stir in the blanched vegetables until heated through. Add the parsley and cream and continue to heat for 2–3 minutes without boiling. Season to taste with salt and freshly ground black pepper.

3 Add the hot pasta to the sauce with the Parmesan and toss through until well combined. Crack a little black pepper over the top, then serve immediately.

pasta We used 375 g (13 oz) farfalle, sometimes referred to as 'bow-tie' pasta because of their shape.

note If you are using fresh broad beans, take them out of their pods before using, then follow the same technique as if you were using frozen—the method of removing the two layers of skin is called double podding.

vongole in white wine

PREP TIME: 20 MINUTES + 1 HOUR SOAKING
COOKING TIME: 20 MINUTES
SERVES 4

1 kg (2 lb 4 oz) baby clams
125 ml (1/2 cup) virgin olive oil
40 g (1 1/2 oz) butter
1 small onion, very finely chopped
6 large garlic cloves, finely chopped
125 ml (1/2 cup) dry white wine
1 small red chilli, seeded and finely chopped
15 g (1/2 cup) chopped flat-leaf (Italian) parsley

NUTRITION PER SERVE: Fat 36.5 g; Carbohydrate 4 g; Protein 37 g; Dietary Fibre 1 g; Cholesterol 108 mg; 2140 kJ (510 Cal)

1 Scrub the clams with a small stiff brush to remove any grit, removing any that are open or cracked, then soak and rinse clams in several changes of water over an hour or so until the water is clean and grit free. Drain and set aside.

2 Heat the oil and 1 tablespoon of the butter in a large saucepan over medium heat. Add the onion and half the garlic and cook for 10 minutes, or until lightly golden—ensure the garlic doesn't start to burn. Add the wine and cook for 2 minutes, then add the clams, chilli and the remaining butter and garlic and cook, covered, for 8 minutes, shaking regularly, until the clams pop open—discard any that are still closed.

3 Stir in the parsley and season. Add the hot pasta and toss well.

pasta We used 375 g (13 oz) spaghetti.

aglio, olio e peperoncino (garlic, oil and chilli)

PREP TIME: 5 MINUTES
COOKING TIME: 5 MINUTES
SERVES 4

185 ml (3/4 cup) extra virgin olive oil
5 garlic cloves, finely chopped
1 teaspoon chilli flakes
3 tablespoons chopped flat-leaf (Italian) parsley
freshly grated Parmesan cheese, to serve

NUTRITION PER SERVE: Fat 41 g; Carbohydrate 0.5 g; Protein 0.5 g; Dietary Fibre 1 g; Cholesterol 0 mg; 1530 kJ (365 Cal)

1 Heat the oil, garlic and chilli in a frying pan while the pasta is cooking. Cook only until the garlic starts to brown, then remove from the heat.

2 Toss the hot pasta and the parsley through the sauce and season well with salt and black pepper. Serve with Parmesan, if desired.

pasta Use 375 g (13 oz) long, thin pasta, such as spaghetti.

notes Because this pasta is so simple, it is important to use good-quality ingredients, especially the oil.

If the garlic is overcooked, it will taste very bitter. It will keep cooking once you remove it from the heat so cook it only until it just begins to turn brown.

Traditionally this pasta is not served with Parmesan because it was a peasant dish, eaten by those who could not afford such luxuries.

walnut and mascarpone

PREP TIME: 10 MINUTES
COOKING TIME: 10 MINUTES
SERVES 4–6 (AS A LIGHT MEAL)

40 g (1 1/2 oz) butter
2 garlic cloves, finely chopped
150 g (5 1/2 oz) walnuts, finely chopped
1 tablespoon finely chopped sage leaves
250 g (9 oz) mascarpone cheese
50 g (1/2 cup) freshly grated Parmesan cheese
1 tablespoon chopped parsley

NUTRITION PER SERVE (6): Fat 39 g; Carbohydrate 2 g; Protein 10.5 g; Dietary Fibre 2 g; Cholesterol 64.5 mg; 1655 kJ (395 Cal)

1 Heat the butter in a saucepan over medium heat, add the garlic, walnuts and sage and sauté for 4 minutes, or until the garlic is golden. Reduce the heat to low and stir in the mascarpone and Parmesan for 2 minutes, or until the cheese has melted into a rich, smooth sauce.

2 Toss through the hot pasta, season to taste with salt and freshly ground black pepper. Sprinkle with parsley, then serve immediately.

pasta We used 250 g (9 oz) rigatoni, a popular tube-shaped pasta with ribbed walls that catch the sauce.

note This is a very rich dish and is not recommended as a main course.

mozzarella, tomato and basil

PREP TIME: 10 MINUTES
COOKING TIME: 15 MINUTES
SERVES 4–6

2 tablespoons olive oil
2 x 400 g (14 oz) cans chopped tomatoes
1 tablespoon tomato paste (purée)
1 teaspoon caster (superfine) sugar
1 teaspoon dried oregano
3 tablespoons torn basil leaves, plus extra, to garnish
200 g (7 oz) mozzarella cheese, cut into 1 cm (1/2 inch) cubes
50 g (1/2 cup) shredded Parmesan cheese

NUTRITION PER SERVE (6): Fat 16 g; Carbohydrate 5.5 g; Protein 13 g; Dietary Fibre 2 g; Cholesterol 29 mg; 920 kJ (220 Cal)

1 Heat the oil in a large frying pan. Add the tomato, tomato paste, sugar and dried oregano and cook over medium–high heat for 15 minutes, or until the mixture thickens and reduces.

2 Add the hot pasta to the sauce with the basil, mozzarella and Parmesan and toss well. Serve immediately, garnished with extra basil.

pasta Use 500 g (1 lb 2 oz) fusilli or other pasta shape.

pictured: walnut and mascarpone

index

Aglio, olio e peperoncino, 60
Alfredo, 7
Amatriciana, 24
anchovies and basil, Broccoli, 15
Anchovy, caper and chilli, 51
Arrabiata, 24
Artichoke, lemon and ham, 40

bacon and pecorino, Cauliflower with, 31
bacon and pecorino, Spinach, 31
basil, Broccoli, anchovies and, 15
basil, Mozzarella, tomato and, 63
Bolognese, 8
Boscaiola, 48
Broccoli, anchovies and basil, 15
butter and shaved parmesan, Sage, 28

caper and chilli, Anchovy, 51
caper, rocket and lemon, Tuna, 27
capsicum, Grilled, 56
Carbonara, 7
Cauliflower with bacon and pecorino, 31
cheeses, Four, 35
Chicken, mushroom and tarragon, 52
chicken, pine nut and lemon, Roast, 16
chilli, Anchovy, caper and, 51
chilli, Crab, lemon and, 11
chilli, Garlic, oil and, 60
Classic pomodoro, 12
Crab, lemon and chilli, 11
Creamy lemon, 40
Creamy mushroom, 48

fennel and pine nut, Sardine, 55
feta, Pumpkin and, 20
Four cheeses, 35

Garlic, oil and chilli, 60
Gorgonzola cream, 35
Grilled capsicum, 56

ham, Artichoke, lemon and, 40

ink, Squid in black, 44

Lamb shank, rosemary and red wine ragu, 32
leek in saffron cream, Prawns and, 19
lemon and chilli, Crab, 11
lemon and ham, Artichoke, 40
lemon, Creamy, 40
lemon, Roast chicken, pine nut and, 16
lemon, Scallop, rocket and, 11
lemon, Tuna, caper, rocket and, 27
Lentil, winter vegetable and thyme, 39

Marinara, 36
mascarpone, Walnut and, 63
Meatball and tomato, 43
Mozzarella, tomato and basil, 63
mushroom, Creamy, 48
mushroom and tarragon, Chicken, 52

Norma, 47

oil and chilli, Garlic, 60
oregano and creamy tomato, Tuna, 27

parmesan, Rocket, fresh tomato and, 51
parmesan, Sage butter and shaved, 28
pecorino, Cauliflower with bacon and, 31
pecorino, Spinach, bacon and, 31
Pesto, 23
Pesto rosso, 23
pine nut and lemon, Roast chicken, 16
Pine nut, sardine, fennel and, 55
pomodoro, Classic, 12
Prawns and leek in saffron cream, 19
Primavera, 59
Pumpkin cream and thyme, 20
Pumpkin and feta, 20
Puttanesca, 4

Quattro formaggi, 35

ragu, Lamb shank, rosemary and red wine, 32
red wine ragu, Lamb shank, rosemary and, 32
ricotta and basil, Zucchini, 28
Roast chicken, pine nut and lemon, 16
Rocket, fresh tomato and parmesan, 51
rocket and lemon, Scallop, 11
rocket and lemon, Tuna, caper, 27
rosemary and red wine ragu, Lamb shank, 32

saffron cream, Prawns and leek in, 19
Sage butter and shaved parmesan, 28
Sardine, fennel and pine nut, 55
sausage and tomato, Spicy, 56
Scallop, rocket and lemon, 11
Slow-roasted tomato, 12
Spicy sausage and tomato, 56
Spinach, bacon and pecorino, 31
Squid in black ink, 44

tarragon, Chicken, mushroom and, 52
thyme, Lentil, winter vegetable and, 39
thyme, Pumpkin cream and, 20
tomato and basil, Mozzarella, 63
tomato, Meatball and, 43
tomato and parmesan, Rocket, fresh, 51
tomato, Slow-roasted, 12
tomato, Spicy sausage and, 56
tomato, Tuna, oregano and creamy, 27
Tuna, caper, rocket and lemon, 27
Tuna, oregano and creamy tomato, 27

vegetable and thyme, lentil, Winter, 39
Vongole in white wine, 60

Walnut and mascarpone, 63
white wine, Vongole in, 60

Zucchini, ricotta and basil, 28